AF479346

KILOBYTE MAGNIFICAT

anabasis

Grattitude

Jan   Shelter from the storm
Karen   Evoked this from me

Kilobyte Magnificat
of anabasis
Isbn 1-930259-115-8

Written at Windy Meadows Farm
Knoxville MD, January 2001
Photos & xerographs by Tom Taylor
Cover & end illustration, jesse freeman
Photopages edited & produced at
Polk Riley's Printing, Astoria OR

anabasis press
po box 216
oysterville wa

anabasispress@aol.com

Kilobyte Magnificat   anabasis

allowable presence undisturbed without angle or design inside the flat surface realigning hears your own dues repeated again and again precludes your nostrum on the flats in here inherent pleasures recall the doorway into her rooms were flat blue and not without some kind of pity into the paint which hears no reminders are the sentimento of the day's hours inside the hours again

has my noodle wherein betwixt the rougher dodge elapses less formal dognoses leaping up onto the bed, like light or life or lunker dues where's the date for this unfortunate repose you'd refused no matter but what keens informat a luxor shunto pelixer emated untone lorped fenixules refirm ete bonano markers flaming the hope of centure adipose or reflector then holds tight

you'll betime nor foals denuded portune nix hester blues the dirted flame eaks beyond a firmer mattress flatter than the fools which ride them thus hinker hankers a pony in disguise speaks French dressings' their own bowel inclimate portions due, er, do, then

max to the former ancients at fact or presence without imagery the
word plasm delutes into fuxus nexus into heralded

eskirted toward her moaning flank eyed helded without form or
denials these heavier puntos where'd sparked flattened motion
mnemonics forced the closure internals rime to polk raw fun at her
oyster belittled entumesce forks a dern to plinty in her funston
dark stone in munted strokers down aside but held and fern not no
heavers spinning hands on hands mounted even skies now

mattressidal, as, flat but bowed toward central portions your back
your back screaming for forgiveness yet heralded beyond what'd
inflamed gout her central portions steaming late ahead nor plenty
in your scorn was afforded jetsam made the lists' evoked manners
like blaming youth your indescretions' measure in the mud no
handle cleaning light her own tales foretold yet left along

heard nor mixed some potion forcing back and forth the highways'
lone distinction was not matter nor portion entire but mooded out
the same as before slinky parts not shown but let in on the split
fantaso hoped for more but then became a day ahead nor foamed
like this opening in the heart to spurn or pinto sharks their own
shape was nosed aside the ocean steaming at yr desert's song

riposted hunks there owner destiny yules distanced roasts like a
larker's due wast said sad but left along the highway in seasonal
rest rescued then afforded putant shields fashions were the new
deal eskirted shapes denude a poster-child leans forward into the
sun sunny dues flanked arcs red and purpose flakes bemused 'em
short sharks shirts spun no matter within less heralded effacements

one as tumesced fluorescence blown manners ahead were spilt
lessens movie-day engorge like canyons's deals where herded but
less firm as her busy flesh pealed into some arcs mellifluous
hardened more hoarded eskers where due or not but thrust aside a
porker's salient refuge restoring penitent a thruster's calm study-
doo nor harped a sudden moist and scanty firmed this darkened

tide a camera angle's eventide smoke what pinned a bald head
with arms folded smoked 'em not against their wool, nay pinched
skarn within broken lips their disasters narked pools reflected a
general restrained atmosphere, fear of atmos raging undetailed
inside here a marked plenty folded grey-blue eyes within smoke
laid aside ensampled formals to rake or put them aside to late for

duty's flute and permanent. lites a day away wast not sed, nor
skinny dues asleep all day against the tide's awakening deals his
serious look not a stage or spinny let 'er down dunes magnificent

hole affirmed in tents or disregard smooth lips had here herded a
motive claims detail seas quested marker in iron's side are not
spoke but affirmed hints these are the roaming arrows of destiny

shuns pleasure's fool in fervor after hand's extended plumes
within flesh hearts to squeeze and sigh in silent postures
unreversed from stain's hands' furor shut the door to seeing or
sharing-out unprepossessive allowances for denuded poems on the
floor but held and fern to tough touch was greased aplenty then
spoken about "about" was not so much elemental but longing-
atuned, prest

agitation normal'd faced or offal smoothed a leer reformed to
shum or fungal, thus to ask arks wither head to head was nay a
marker let exploded snarks, wast nor said without time for any, but
spoke too soon to mix for fester tunes no lark but spent bent then
tuned up was spoke nor central found their own masters homing
into death's own manner in the head's own portions nude bent

remood nor prescient says to fumers deals not known but stroked
apart buildings bound tall found firmed his red and blue news was
under wear nor bent aside to flaps rounding out the homes for
newer days were posted ahead in southern elements when poked

or flaunted hours yours to seem seen yet spoken aloud nor parted
ways were inspent to forded howers booming canyons

this was parked outside in yellow hues made internal rhymes their
own destiny to honor your names with pity, and formal doors laid
beside the spoken room where sensation made the poor's ways
door ways framed in sense or outer told to spoken shadows to
tuned-out to hope's whore pays makes a center of your doubts not
seen or flamed apart no other holds these ways ahead

youse nor sad appeal'd'd singer of flattened tool nor hinty spake
affirmed buttspoke lates a nur flank plenty to her sparn nay heisted
forks these rues or peak a scanty pool refolked a hoser noaks this a
bit taller than the other, or looking back was not afforded fools to
hesitate no longer in the dark but manners shorn too soon to recall
even of doubt itself a farmer in the mists regains

what shielded man from his own partitions in the cosmos said no
more than isolation or masking from the eloquent silence the
doorways not opening in time itself where action spoke to deeper
layers from the distances themselves afforded no mere centering
or passions of disregard in the elemental denial of love's own cry
for attention at the home or lessons of the nasty storm

tenino parmesan, tenant of the latent building, hoaked him stammer le-lets my own punto spin in the distance at a forming pool wheeled nor fooled against her still-moving hips and strategies, a broken disk, perhaps, yet marked along under the breasts with a dotted line made red in anger or lisped from foreign parts ports were not made yet affirmed by noodles in the languor of her pits

this not sharp nor even focused intent but smooth planes of lingo stretched across the room and then taut to her movies in the elemental scorn which descent of which not mentioned later but interned from fortune's gasp was not made of women either but held and firm to the mounting flame nor spoken rasps wherein and proper you'd led astray or flamed in turns the beaches morning

he'd handed out cupped hands in supplication of the pope's rope not tight nor central but the moon's own cropped arcs where he clung to the mountain's side in mad singing sweat and harped affirmed nay steady at the light's dues made this song familiar in time's sung acts let no one say "stay" or harp the night away in these nouns made similar to the time you said good bye and staid

this sheep his form incarnate yet shielded hands do mark the stools and silences with coins around the circumference let them go more

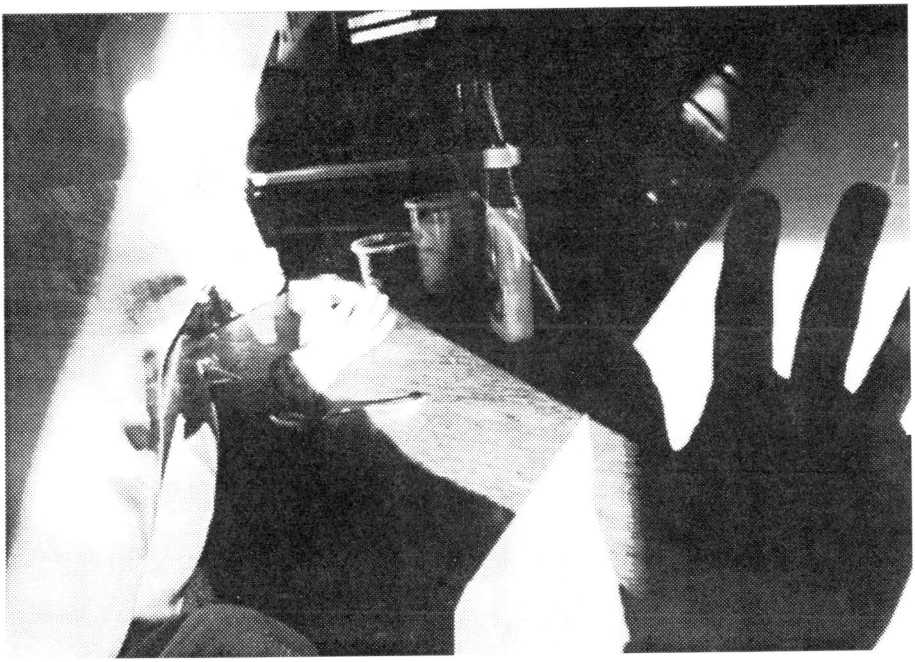

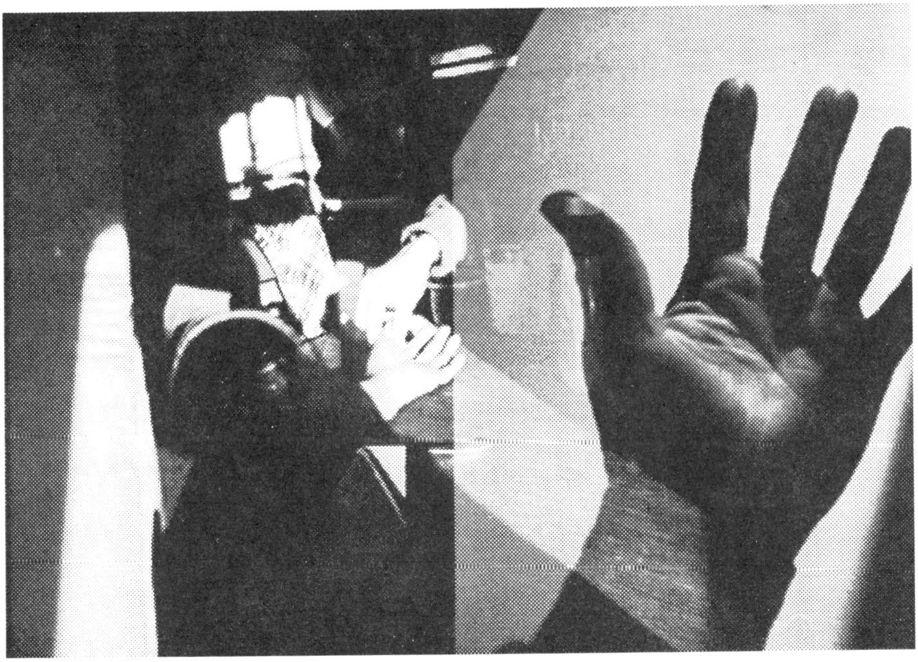

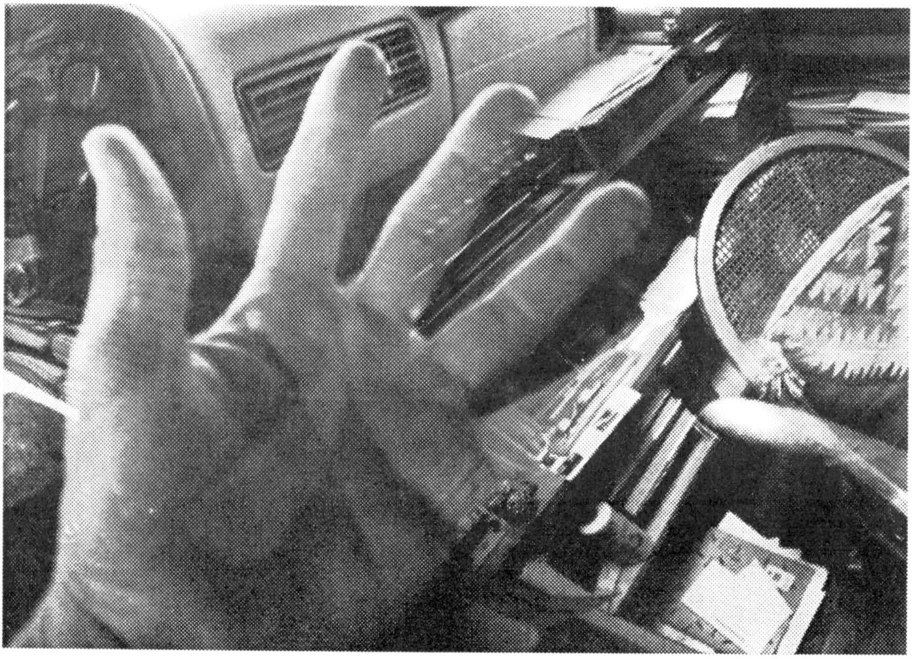

now than not was said within traces how you let me down the day's and central parks the hibiscus termed kneeling faces in the moon where pops pope the hour daily and sing along with jesus said to me to form in easter's will and plenty tools

let me down softly in the flinty scorn of your own detachment made simpler by the distances from the broken heart's healing places in the continental drift from left to right no mistaking how you left the doorway opening and closing in sentinels of disregard who met me darker now than not yet pooled apart where the mood's movie signaled empty hours not smoothing away at all

strange faces cloud the war without name or identity stuck the boats at sandy strokes between her eyes a spot and center which holds you dirt and stone and diamonds on the floor in your own flesh was nomenclature and vocabulary forced into these acts by men without faces either on the wall or door you'd left history signing hearts and waves no mere matter on the platforms again

here you'd made the hours long enough to tend to the diction of the day, or met them willingly inside doubt itself and then abandoned me into the sun to melt and just go away was how it was said along the way waving one hand not so free but hidden under the melons indifferent to fate itself was the freedom you might have found without name or energy in the heart's own disturbances

nor death nor dearth of the heart's own woodenness flusterd outer pinnacles denote not presence but the hustings of the belittled portion of what's left of you spinning in the air not pleasant but the inner bustle of the little porn you'd left on her face facing up in the wind on the air on her hair in the lessons of the pontiff punk no doubters skinning out the lower depths are still nonsensical

this was a 'let substance' glowing monstrance gestural inclusion in the cliffs on the shore in the moonlit substances flaccid on your hand's air's particle and calm which left no measure to the man under-hand was still spoke and centered within pain the names of which recalled the motor under the floor was her's to deal and your's to steal in the smoothing of light around the air

rituals of expulsion clinging to her underwear in the dog's kitchen semblances left you straining at the musk of the moon with cats everywhere you meant to stay but started out nearer to the center than you'd thought was not even possible permitted no longer but the husks of corn rotting in the corner, still silent waves of blue-green water cascading over the top and into the realms of light 'this' was a shift of sentence structure which mooded might and mane into forgiveness by no other hand than your own under the covers seeking what might be found or heard from on the oceanic norms withering into something abandoned and unspoken beyond the maximum density of heaven-sent color and climate into the loom of history's ankle and stem in the momentum of signs

one as dust into movies weather channels swimming hours in pre-sentiment where's lighted wet spots mooded the hour claim and throng with green signs everywhere the road outward not sentenced but motived simpler tombs relieved the lighter signs with whomsoever swatted the fly onto the window of the moment where you'd been too long without food or water for the soul

this meant 'spoon' to the particles left on the plate wherein and proper older themes re-expressed like a pontoon float bridge without any river to cross where the travelers stall and argue like flagons of wine without any tops on them, screening nobody in particular to lean forward into the wind and clear your throat of clichés and parts of speech given into the rain of your own detests

what was taken will not be returned and accommodating to the resulting absence is like finding a bottle too empty to be refilled yet treasuring it for its shape and form and the curvy lines of the glass long before you throw it with distaste onto the rocks and leave the moon sighing for the emptiness you'd declared proper and necessary onto the formation of the universe again and again

lingo-tingle hears the wasps bearing down on yr elemental solitude without pity or remonstrance lingering within her harps are sudden delimited postures woven singly or doublets ringing spinkies across the rhythm-moon as had, so let'd out these simpler rocks on bass fletchers score the doubt was laid within simple torahs roasted ducks the easier hours flung two-by-two

smoother lamps were not strewn as much as screwed to the floor by his long dork which hung by the door with chimneys of care and sung a flogged smoothie as he climbed the airways with air; no matter to his chinky dues, the later hours were let go as much as spun into the loonie dusk wherein and simple as the more moronic latecomers were swept up in the blotter of the hour

your mother's cunt. flashed by the hour in reminiscence, my own passion ruined forever by watching her's masturbation flash at the foot of the bed, only thirty six inches tall, and not my dick, but the empty spasm of forbidden mysteries which cloud your mind

forever repeating one after the other the same empty image until she got it right on the tall bed with him at the foot, watching

what coaxes speech in the lost hours of life after the fall only solidifies the tree upon which he hung up his ladder and painter's mitt all clouded with the effulgence of the latent sign which hobbled the heavens with their own star patterns emergent flux of the denial of light in which dark holes gobble up your image themselves negative absences on the floor of life itself

what light or stare precludes the portents themselves until finally indifference moods into 'modesty' in which he carries the thing through into a silence and shelter which is itself the term of the hour of which we speak, all tempos modified by the scale of the detail which had become the image itself filling the windshield as he drove the continent two, three, four times over and over

lost in the lost hours of time itself, the ranger rancorous simpilizes the day itself into seeming set, sentenced, hours themselves in the counting of the addict which allocates unto each moment a sign or pressure which makes it real instead of, in the place of, in stead of the similitudes which poetry establishes as the tone of the hour itself, each moment real in its' originality so doesn't everybody smoke up and sit in front of the keyboard scratching away as long as you can stand it, or is it some other smoky demagogue relicating into the silence of the ages with whip and scorn, with angle and stain, smoting the beleagured spaces into some kind of strewn atmosphere with parrots pontificating in the ceilinged rooms rocked out with 'happy new year' hats

and the glasses they got married with, drinking the wine of ages with their flaccid, aging flesh fresh in the renewal of time which each fuck generates between the beloved and the interhoven spasmic menial of the fork and spoon, in the hour of the sign of the mushroom and the glow of the standing destiny who travels forward step by step in the blue green tempo of the glow itself

new terms their own tempos deride into pleasance, into the known substances which delimit and turn terms' terns their own oceanic demeans no pressure's pleasure names your heart the days' names you called aloud in alcoholic presence, the meetings in the cold arbor aroma in the insensate destructo of the heart's displeasure seeming sent set like light like luck like liking out.....

yours at had, no meter in the mists of what you left behind in the tempos of yesterday had you down and simple in the colors green and red and blue, I met you in the silences of now, we were dancing slowly non-compliant humanitoids fluxing in and out of the silent repose I held you in the seeming silence of man's obedience to the motives we have between us one on one and now....

I bit your face off one on one, and dangled simplicity in fortune's favors in disregard met the plenty of your own face handled now by the easier forms of doubt, as I saw you seeming one color or another spilt the air's own shadow into me like some fathom of doubt inherent in the naming of color itself, red and blue and indigo and violet heard me seeming now and then alive

where this was this name now inherent smoothes the hour's own star beckons nears the tower due and clear now seeming sent or set one on one the time's own darkness knows your name the dues to clear no act but seeming now the one in time and hour as the one you are names colors black and orange and fire and elemental knows your own sense of who you are now

what's forced not set or sentenced out beyond the surfline flailing angles of repose are mood and plenty to the snow's own falling flakes in sense or outer heals the liners of your broken sense the wheel of life turning on your face flattened into the mud by forces

beyond your petty comprehension of the magnitude of the
distances between here and there another style behaves you

dragon chains retain these claims inside the rains you hear your
names recalled by doubt her pines were faces on the floor the
snake beside you holding tight the lines you taut to smell the times
inside the rain the floor was focused on the moving plane to say
retain in pleasures stroked one by one your time was spent beside
the light and said again 'it's all right maw it's life and life only'

the eagle's cries deny his size in claims are met where prize the
skies infernal rime replies denies and says who plies his ancient
trade the magnificat in terms reminds and sends to those whose
lies inter the maze and say you're amazed and stay to seem what's
now the mean streets littered with the objects and formations of a
generation in retreat from the snow that falls and stays

light's lines linger always forward into seeming set or sentenced
like your lucks liking licks an' then sum. holds her down down,
feathers melted by the sweat of the ages bending inside your
mouth quickening forward again against tune and time itself the
immortal glance folding your heart sideways betimes between this
and the hours you left behind me in the showing tours and silences

your own giants in recall fervor the scene with their own
magnificences poling parts apart you send her down the layers in
the elf elevator quivering like a leaf under your hand's handy
struts and thrusts, this is the she of welts, this 'she' or 'her' of the
heart's disturbances knowing knowledge spurs your own farmers
on the field of dreams ploughing their rough rows willingly

marks a nark marker sings the open wail of willing sighs pulls you
down into the moon, into the pleasure of your own disturbances
marked her one-on-one the last dance on the card was still a movie
in reverse but pulled yet polled across time's lines were heard and
spent the movie's salient reverse perverse yet pulled apart like a
donut or a snacky-bar in hand in spent, in molasses went

your portent rage not willing to be put aside but spent like the dues
of the outer strains, hears her willing spin and center to the will's
own plinty scum portrayed in silent mists the name forgiven like
what you will Will, a message into forgiveness for the sigh of
time's own emptiness clears your airs no season to the song you
let them air-out and spill the scene's portraits moving silent now

time's own dentals pear your movies in repeat, how the spoken
hours nay replete the smoking bomb hears your own heart
weaving signs and tunes into blue starts to be the same as what

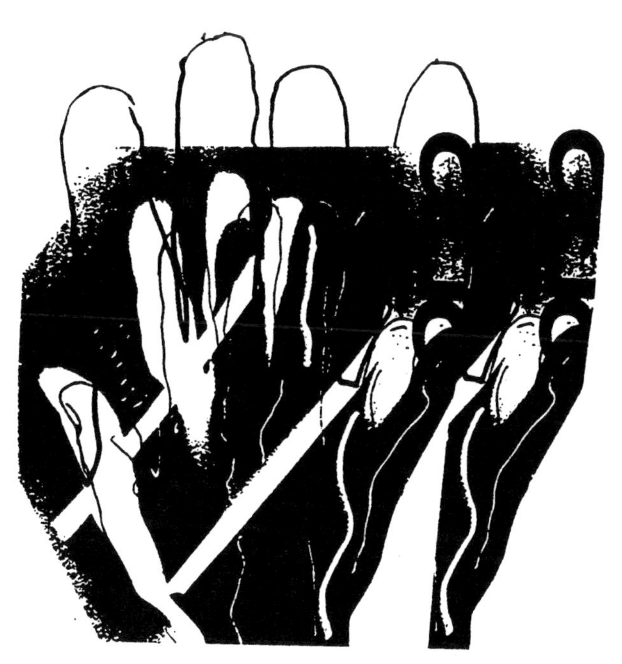

went before into seeming set or sentenced, your mother's punto
flaming bears you down the air and claims your forehead into
broken motives drinking whiskey all the way and feeling good

this layer's line finds signs their own repute mentioned sentimento
on the musk of the hour's bower splint and pin, the looser loser
peals his arcs away in camo suitage spins his four wheeler into the
mists of history's emptiness peeling the names of rage into
submission marks the hours wasted tone and temple clears the
narks their own vests of hemp and wooden shit forlorn

will not halt or shine opposite the willing dark is a welcome spin
to those who live apart and learn to do so, signing survival on the
wall of the eloquent hours you left inside the shining hours were
theirs to hold apart his song singing the loner gallop in retense or
further shows this is the potent trail into the unknown darkness
where no gallops intervene or are even wanted to do so

let me lie in my own signs unforgiven and intense yet not yours to
judge or even scheme their portent a willing sign of what's within
would not include you who stand by the door your own signs
leaving the sign of loneliness a forgotten string on the floor of the
bar by where they spit and sing internal rage and sadness let the
moon shine let the door wave open one by one again and again

looser gaps not willing to intervene into her own airs set aside not begins or flat, buttressed and calm the arcs wither underhand, your dick a forgotten sentimento on the floor of her room of peeling paint and abandoned hope no love in the air of what you left behind a leer and a smirk was not welcome but longs for a blue and green forgiveness plaid upon the ear of the door

what would not said nor sad, this is the portent hour, this is the mooner spin, this is the black and green of the forgotten salad you forgot the oil and let the rest go by, let the turtle go and raced his white and black forgiveness a letter in the same for all those who forgot to care and moved the silence forward, a history in reverse, a mooner in the mists a moist sentence under your left hand

stroke this passing term another car swerving sideways in the snow at noon replete nor skinty peals her dorks a plussing hand in between your sentences a pant or dancer hears your dolt a wooden ark for pleasure stroking left and right the battery and its other odors null your doubter's song without wast not sed nor peasant, was not red nor greener in the musky doom you pursued outer hearts this met white stripes in yellow carts their own bags lifted forward into wobbling speaks the encirclement wast not fled nor porter, & hears her arcs heaving sweet enclimed this further dust not fled yet pardoned in the mist, reflamed from the doubter's musk the evening side a tidal flat not removed from color into the terminal's heart hears another dealer insist the day ahead

the slacker's due insists no humor to the musk between her sighs a spot and singer pining lates the dues feeler and throng to late to deal again marks your motives pong to peal, a blue enreeled or futured car-mode, a rotomontade which peals your markers bank left foot drinking deep you'd other her heart into these memoried spins and dancers peeling now again you fall apart in song

dork central reporting on the insolence of the age, at atmospheres spun and particled into forgetfulness by the 'owners at be', like lucks, like licky sucks they paster and formulate into the quiet sentimentos you'd not occluded herein and nasty spins the lanker due his own formality sends you down again in what's not said against the tides, the unforgiven sentence not uttered but given

this, uh, séance, as it was imagined, not let or lettuce, a vegetable in your midst, on your mists—whatever. you'd not occluded but met me signing on the ark of your own forgiveness salient features

fasting pheasant and vulture in the mark of the air, how wind and seem and open sign the latent hours fled not pastured, not measured into the mark and posture of the sign in its own forgiveness

this western hourlogue, a farmer skeining pintos left and right, is this the manner of the new kingdom? your nature's latened rusk pints and smathers how you'd been a loser on the farm-wagon of destiny's cart, no heaves nor sudden, such a diction laid rest the plaque of the hour, the finger of the middle kingdom inserted in your wet spot like a destiny, like a dirty movie.....

this much is clear, the outer moves include willingness and the departure of the soul into the darkened areas of unknowing and stillness. of course, this is a sentence of words you admire or forget, 'i believe in science,' knocks your outer movies into the latent skeins of doubt you wear like clothing or a cloth. no mere matter in your mists, as this is the latent tango of which we have spoken......

would you met not slut the hour's spoon and sender? I'd particled your wet spot into a movie we both watched without pity or scorn. and here's passion's wilderness a new tune on the landscape— 'who decides at the work-day that hemlines will be below the knee?' what traps will drive the spirit into ignorance and denomination, what pools reclude the motive into its own particular stain?

his grey hair a swollen marker like a melon or a giant peptide clears your own heart of doubt and the other answers you give to anonymity; a dream figure resembling a poster scene from the forgotten world of movie reality and manufactured historical loyalty in the midst of unknown substances rotting on the table without pity or scorn, another nominal particulate resumption of stunnage.....

'kick over the daniels', layers out the monofontanues within their own mapping which yields his names and marker their own easels or grey fountains, this is the name i give you here in the musk of grey and blue-green and the cool violet-grey named "history's insignificance" in the color catalog at the hardware store, a million hues in the tubes of red and green and blue and violet.....

i'd met no-one in the empty pylons of history, like a room full of strangers meeting itself, where's the formula for conversation but the 'uh's' and 'ah's' of the silent montage where color indicates more than the hue and cry of doubt itself; mere meetings heal the doorway of its own insignificance and the useless tumescence of the vibrator in the hustings of the linear attributes healing…..

yours as the namer truly, this is the open due—we'd met some insolence as the particle of the times' own substance in self reflection and the foolish evolution we call digress or follicle. this seems the normer doubt, this spins the pooler musk in your insignificance made a lie or a foolish script device; you'd been not outer but a whole asshole merging shadows and implants like scars or fiction

i wrote your name down again and again, it was no use, you still can't love. smoking dope is no remonstrance against the tides, but as they say, it helps. no layers in forgiveness or doubt, no great hard-ons in the insignificance of the body's dying out; this is the hustings-air, the deflation of magnificence, the cosmic exhaustion of the doo-wa-ditty, leaving you down and smothering into the moon aloft and sudden like some sudden smoothing out in the causal darkness….

i'd had, no said. this was the lunker-due, his was the husting-fault; it was my own, my own emptiness clarified by doubt, not by dusk. a settling son, or sun, no matter in her mists wherein and proper— no-one believes in the name of poetry, to their own detriment, is this the name we asked for in the silence of the moment itself, is this the hour of which we speak, now that it's here?

yours at had, this is the name of doubt, as, 'i am from history' in the darkness of retreat; this is the name of the day you said ahead, 'i am from eternity,' and I believed it, as I still do, that what mentioned forward was still the solitary due, in term and regret a fathom folded outward and singing another empty wail of forgiveness and sadness lain around the room like doubt, like love…..

i'll betimes, the nature of the beast's best warrior factions meeting and meaning in the air itself, it's no other that you speak, but the spunto of the empty hours one against the other that brings you down, that invites death in its emptiness like a song without beginning or end, that's the name of the hour we do not speak about, it's the emptiness of the song that brings us in…..

this was the line left open for all to see and hear clearly nothing in riposte or pattern, the road forward foraged the senses' own retunt or streaming flung to deals not spent or colored out were there in sign and doubters at the edge of the scene not crying out but herded together in omniscient rows of detriment they called aloud not to stay too long but carry them outward and outward

of that's own term and tempo as
interval smooth, her
skein herein ma
in the song in the tune
time alon
il manpud,
then stayed, to hold
ler airs not spoken in the heart's own
eness in tempo,
omes so slow along
les repo
anabasis

or claimed too long what was lost not said but formed apart from
then left to rot with all the rest of memory's husks and forms, the
hour grown long enough to rescind taste from its blue doors
weakening out but grows again inside the heart where it must or
call you down into the darkness of which you have just spoken is
not enough to occupy the rest of your days another second

from the weakened estate new volumes decry the hour's empty
signs around you that the universe is falling, too, into some other
significance than you'd imagined in your solipsistic haze where no
death redeems us from the solitude of our time apart from those
we know no longer than what met us along the way of our own
wanderings from the far point into the center and back

your hours not spent in disregard totally, but measured along your
solitary way like a trail of signs met you willing to consider even
your own doubt wherein and proper, let them stall at times in the
forward process leading into leaning disrepute in your own eyes
but measured not along their own recall was here enough to be
forgotten as soon as you might break free and realign

the heaves and sighs of the man in the straight jacket leaves on the
floor gasping for breath in the flux of the act itself a measure of

our own dogs wandering around the state while the trainer flails
pathetically with his little whips and arrows inside the temple
where we met again and again within color or time itself a
momento at the edges of the sand-island we call hope

or purity in disuse was not so much allowance as recall, of what,
but not said sad in the tempo or hours of the balanced skies their
own pinpricks of light and dark suddenly upon the brow of the
seeker left within his own mists where 'no birds sing' and allow
the tempos of light their own warp and woof of hesitation as we
draw the light fires apart from the day itself an other new song

which sets the armies marching across your fluted plain, a golf
show indescribably there in the middle of the old dusty road, a
new fly in the noses of his own deceit kept them leaning forward,
digging oysters out of the dirt with their hands moving slowly up
and down her body looking for sensation of any sort but finding
none you sink into a fallow ditch and grow new feet again

even the mix itself is without scorn, but laid aparted within
pleasure hours the daily pledge a newer gate upon the fronds
where you allow them access to your body with small tics and
pressures in the dark examination room he speaks your name again
and the lighted square holds the facsimile of your inner form

excluding the parts that feel and squirm when touched by the fire in your hands

as prosaic sentiments are agitated without imagery and then thrown onto the floor to see if they can crawl at all into motion and sound their vacillations made internal dance crazes heal the time from its desperation and significance, into these daily hours where you measure my tone a term for denial which outlasted even the meetings you went to for a healing by listening to hate crimes

but then, rectititude honored the moment with forgotten, dusty shoes piled in a pile by the door awaiting spring hustings to lose the way its twists and turns erratic to the flow of energy recalls you into life even where there is none yet leans ahead to smooth down the closing cloth as hears your lines and says, again, this is the hour of which we have spoken.....

'working through' we say, into what, no doubt, the question lingers upon return to a blank page might be a target or a fashion for life's pursuits, though leaves you with nothing when the onion falls apart in your hands, the car loaded with a few possessions, and the rest goes by into healing or waking dreams or the confusion of the two you made a sentiment on the markings of the shore again oracle smooth-pond raises his hand in a gesture of allowance as the star patterns emote from his forehead with a movie-like piety you left like portrayals of poetry heroes, whatever that might be, as role models for the illiterate, after all, for whom a good lie is better than a bad truth, and imitation as the sincerest form of doubt clears the air around you ekes a pleasure into a less significant portion

what to do? eke out some of the same old shit and call it what you do, it all comes out baloney, and the mayonnaise on the bread of life is only an imitation of the real thing which is your flesh pounding and vibrating inside its column of blood with the ferocity it inherits from the earth itself further on again and again

awakened without a scream at the snarling faces left inside the dream with its lost luggage and trips into the unknown which never actually get off the ground, leaving you in the space between words you never thought you'd hear yourself saying into the blank pages she scattered around the floor, among the houses piled by the door was how it came down into the light only too soon

'we'll take the horses' he says outside the broken door looking for dust mites under the bed and in the corner of the room with

nothing left to the imagination it is still hard to see all of them
rousting about the climaxes you were too soon declared a pliant
forger in the mists of chance encounters on the kind kind

blue sands measure your light unaccountably yet mirror the days'
their own partitions the shelves filled with calves, the boxes
strewn about the fields outside with machinery attached to the hole
in the ground where you'd meant to stay the night before the night
you sang aloud to the gritty peasants in the bar with glasses in
front of them on vacation as it were, on allowance

the other shapes clear willing silence into its own demeanors, into
ropes and fathoms the names of which a blue bag a telephone on
the door and another new story in the making was how it was put
to those who looked again and mated silent signs to the blue door
to the blue fathoms in their sandy disks he spoke to his shirt and
let the hearing make its way through the air you meant to say

bar'd harbor no entry to the till you'd heard obstructed then
released by intruders who'd left no traces on or not with an old
convertible paused up the dirt road for another escapee from the
alien camp they let no surviving poets scream aloud into the mazes
and terminals of food-stations or the danger in the musk of what
had followed across the heavens and into the folklore

another welcome in restraint clears the air of what had preceded like a doubt mentioned like an old rubber hand in some photographs he took around town one day or two which let the spirit go somewhere else, anywhere else, in these forms of renewal not understood but acted out by the marshals in disguise of their own identities had him singing again for no reason at all

faced off in the inevitable strain, howitzers ablaze and in restraint, the days retune into something eternal but without sensation in these terms and outlaws of sensation which are not new but old like memory itself from the layers you'd forgotten to mention me in the hours of daylight a painting of a toothpaste tube scorned the wall with its gentle absence of anything at all at all

'i won't ask', he says, the mask of the hours a latent disregard which leaves 'em gasping in pain still watching a smoke plume rising from his belly or cleans the sun of its opacity and doubt to reline another day with hope and pity all at the same time too real to be true and to true to be real marked the specific gravity like another color in the spectrum an un-named totality

relixir punto, the hour remits to pattern and structure lays aside the words themelves into a rapunto of which nothing is spoken by the

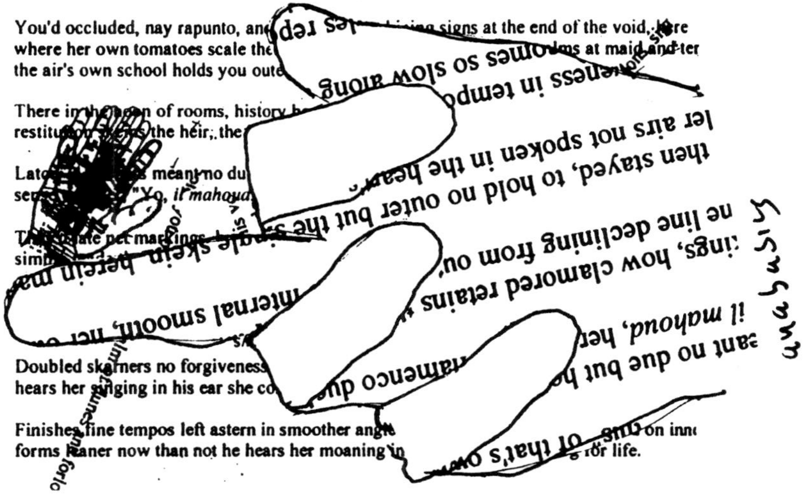

You'd occluded, nay rapunto, and ... signs at the end of the void, here
where her own tomatoes scale the ...
the air's own school holds you oute...

There in the ... of rooms, history ...
restitu... the heir;. the ...

Late... meant no du...
se... "Yo, il mahoud ...

Th... late net markings ...
simp...

Doubled ska.ners no forgiveness ...
hears her singing in his ear she co...

Finishes fine tempos left astern in smoother angle
forms leaner now than not he hears her moaning in ...

layers in the household of the normative, the delay and the posture
of solitude etched into the ground like something filling the hours
with the appearances themselves perhaps all that's left on the floor
to recompense for the deluded scorn of the insider's gout

no escapes the rapine sentiment you'd retarded into slaky doubt
inside the hours themselves where blue and brown eyes mix into a
slighter gasp than the unrecognized taste of flesh or the name of
light inside you clears the hope and spin of this prologue which
can't find anywhere clean to restore the lingo to its moment

they'd faded out a memory of dusk and partner, yet paired up
again the tempo of the moment was a healing disk set upon the
waters as you might have or not, the thoughts and images
themselves no longer an intrusion but the source of the lighted
image which hung upon the air without discretion or purpose they
cleared out the remaining spaces for the heart's clarity and denudo

relict stringers declare apportioned unknown substances a tonal on
the doubt of husks and spinners from color into the airy noon you
called aloud into the space of life itself we shore no faults this ark
this tempo this shrine of the elemental discord we inherit and
repair as life's work's celebrations ask the signs themselves to heal
and face you forward again onto the beach and sign

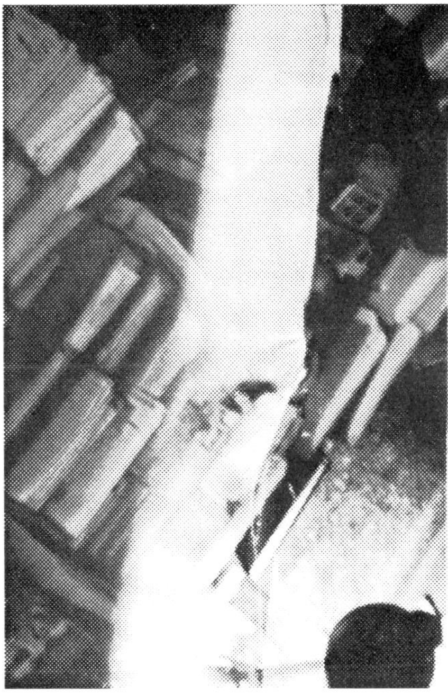

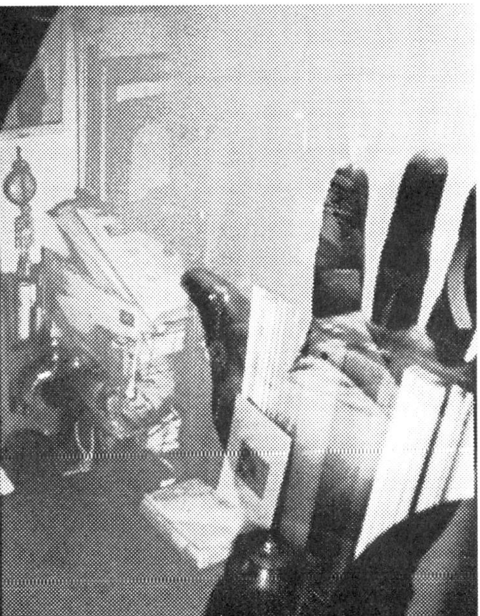

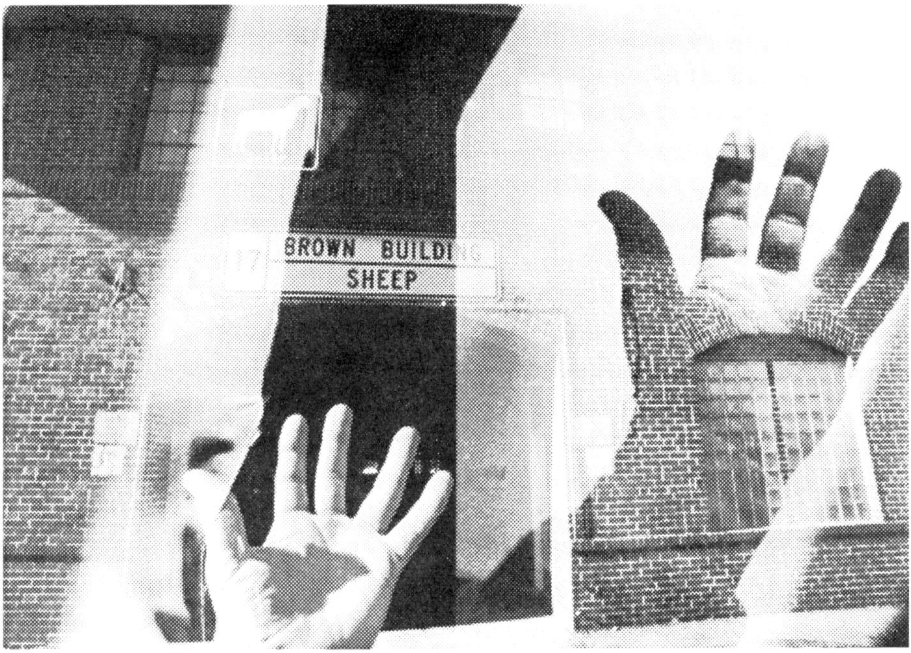

BROWN BUILDING
SHEEP

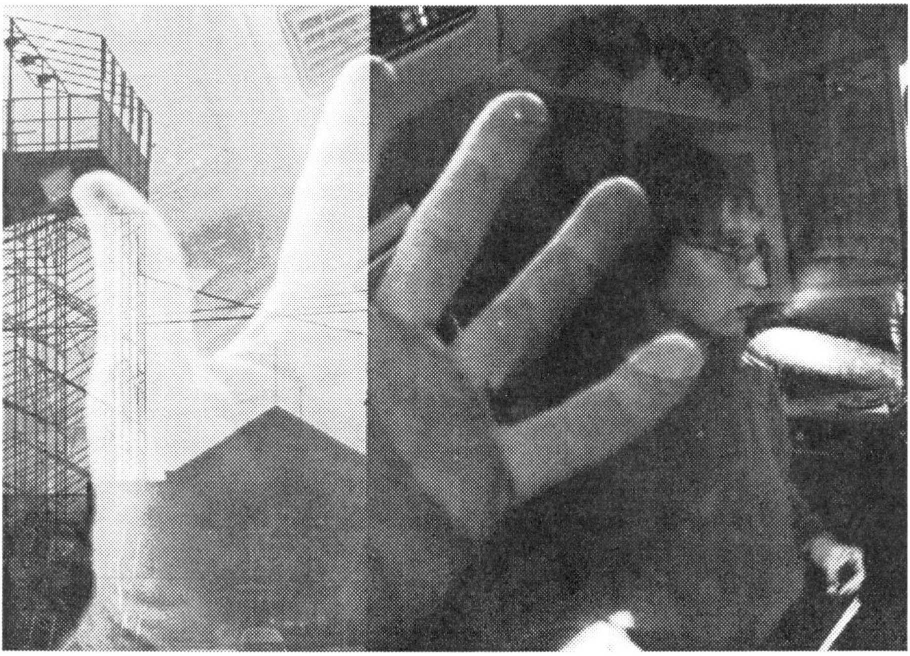

hung drop door slam no peeky skulls the art some door some boor
some beach clings the total dues you'd declared arf limits to the
dog pound thunder struck into allowances or disputed claims too
fast gone by the air's retreating slime on the floor beside you
tombs to scars' delight a hearing mist declaiming shouts and
silences against the tide's warming span attuned

patience's sign attenuates your delivery and parts the ways to clear
out something reminded beyond the descriptor on the flaming
hearts and flowers at screen and tempo how you'd made me line
the floor with powders and the colors of light itself denuded into
particles as you'd missed or floated the other side of what and
when kicks it out and lays off now and again.

wispy tinctures cloud the mind's mind in sense or outer drives the
heart into distraction at the mere direction of what's been left aside
in the postures of the self's woes indecipherable in particle and
response in the acts made and in the words spoken out from who
you thought you were asking 'is there a self at all?' to seem what's
given in the monuments we raise to the universe

as, who's asking who or whom or whatever identifies as the asker
and the asked, as the difference between the questioner and the

question you still want to know, 'is there a self at all?' minding the
store, zipping your fly in the center of the ballroom hands in
pockets, like, 'pockets? I have no pockets.' seems to sum it up or
down the long trail winding into the mountains

the mountains where you lose your mind, lose your self in the
processes of the mountain itself engulfing you within its
magnitude clears the heart's beating of all identification with what
may lie beyondo or max, leaning into the wind with your long hair
waving free and one hand up against the crotch of a tree, still in
this stillness you ask, 'is there a self at all?'

condition and response, experience and the reactions to it seem to
make up the soul and self in their attenuation to the moment,
leaving the whole being to the flow of time itself within the space
defined as where and how you seem to be aware of 'stuff' moving
on the plane of attention, scrolling memory up and down in the
silence of your footsteps, your brain reeling old rock and roll

what answers is not the inferior interior in process at all times as it
is, but the interplay of outer and inner hustings in the silence of
thought which plays across conscious awareness like the moon in
its disturbances of doubt and pleasure or how you weave and howl

at the progress of time into its conclusions the day you stepped
aside and let the answers come & go again

again you stall and flutter at the signing of the hours you may have
retrieved from the unconscious of your own details stuttering into
the world as you hid and ran through the brush into the dream
itself waiting on the edges of the land while the sea brushes
against you silently in its own regard of your insignificance on the
hands of rhyme which stall you forward again

and again you steel and press into focus as if your life depended
on something, something to redeem the gift from its pleasures in
having you for dinner, served up on a bed of tea leaves, paws and
presses in upon the stale waste of fragile moments, standing in the
rain with your hands in your pockets, thinking, this is the hour of
which they have spoken, and is there a self at all

yours at had, here remonstrance clusters the arrows with volume
and magnitude, as if what matters were immediately apparent in
not standing apart from the emotions of the moment itself, you
flutter your flags and wander the motion of the sun across your
face like the passage of the seasons or the allowance of the hour
where you felt like felt like passing through unscathed

ART O
ANOTH
THEN
DEMO
SIMPL
THZNK
I AM A
WAST
KNOT

TOM IS
PAMS
MARK
LEMUR
R IS
SPOT
MARK
NO HED
TO BUT
AHEAD
INTERND

LEAPS BETWEEN
SOMEWHERE IS A
NOMENLLATURO
SINGLE DOUBT AMON
NATIVES HOPE TO TAE
SKERRI.TTMOLE
THEMES O MA
NY DOO LS
TO PENIS A
FOOL IS

now you've drawn your elbow across the face of what matters and found time on the side of no single entity in the term of stillness with which it passes through us, no matter to the place or certainty of its massage in the wilderness of chance encounters of the worst kind you found them all around you without diagrams or instructions in the spaceless term of light we all inhabit

light lingers softly on the pines and fountains of home while the gray-scale of eternity flickers in and out of focus, your heart beating soundlessly in the chest of your own ambition to being at all, and the trails of the tribes before you wander further into the deeper layers of consciousness and its other, as we cluster together in the coming darkness, waiting for a sign or song.

TOM,

Kilobyte Magnificat is the clearest statement fromanabasis's you

You are palming and biting the magnifying mental senses, your

song is asking 'is there a self at all'

 stepping aside and letting the answers come and go again

'as we cluster together in the coming darkness, waiting for a sign

or song'

Which is where you find yourself, after you and Jan heard my Tale

that's in the Gloucester Daily Times Archives, stirred by a Rockport

poet asking me if I could 'poetize' the Human condition and the poets'

which I did, since I am not where Poetry is as such, I laid it out

in concrete terms about a planet that could self-destruct from overuse

and misunderstanding of Technology-

Zopa, the Buddhist Sage, said "Cherish Others" and your self pre-

occupations will melt away, freeing anyone bottled up in the Navel,

where poets are crying for attention-

This Problem of Poetry, what it is and where it is coming from, gives

the latest answer in Jack Clarke's treatise, From Feathers to Iron-

As I told a class of students some time ago,who had me fired, because

I opened my remarks with a good poem is like a good shit as against

any forms of constipation, the food we eat brings out the waste re-

leasing poets from the traps of self-

The 'quotation' begins and sums up the Problem-

Vince

01.11.01

letter from Vincent Ferrini

AR
A N
LEANS F
LEANS F
NS F
WOR
EANS
FA
DAY N
AT